My Healthy Body

DIGESTION

Jen Green

ALADDIN/WATTS
LONDON • SYDNEY

© Aladdin Books Ltd 2003

Produced by:
Aladdin Books Ltd
28 Percy Street
London W1T 2BZ

ISBN 0–7496–4960–7

First published in
Great Britain in 2003 by:
Franklin Watts
96 Leonard Street
London
EC2A 4XD

Editor:
Katie Harker

Designer:
Simon Morse

Illustrators:
Aziz A. Khan, Rob Shone,
Ian Thompson

Cartoons:
Jo Moore

Certain illustrations have
appeared in earlier books
created by Aladdin Books.

Printed in UAE
Medical editor:
Dr. Hilary Pinnock

Dr. Pinnock is a GP working in
Whitstable, Kent. She has written and
consulted on a wide variety of medical
publications for all ages.

Contents

Introduction

Did you know that food and fluids give you energy and help your body to grow and look after itself? This special process occurs in your digestive system, which transforms the food that you eat into part of you! When you swallow, your food enters a series of tunnels where it is broken down so your body can absorb the goodness it contains. This book tells you all you need to know about your digestive system and how to keep it in good shape for a healthy body.

Medical topics

Use the red boxes to find out about different medical conditions and the effects that they can have on the human body.

You and your digestion

Use the green boxes to find out how you can help improve your general health and keep your digestive system in tiptop condition.

The yellow section

Find out how the inside of your body works by following the illustrations on yellow backgrounds.

Health facts and health tips

Look for the yellow boxes to find out more about the different parts of your body and how they work. These boxes also give you tips on how to keep yourself really healthy.

The digestive system

We all need to eat food to live. Food gives you energy and helps your body to grow, maintain and repair itself. Your digestive system is designed to get as many nutrients from your food as possible. The human digestive system includes the stomach, which processes food. Some animals, like cows (right), need four stomachs because they eat grass and hay, which are difficult to digest.

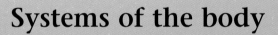
Digestion

Systems of the body

Our bodies are often described in terms of separate systems, each with a different job to do. However, each body system is dependent on another to work to its full potential. Your digestive system extracts nutrients from your food and transfers them to your circulatory system to be carried to all parts of your body.

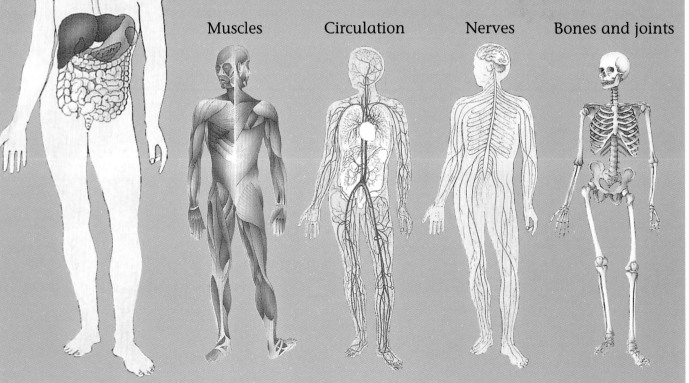

Muscles   Circulation   Nerves   Bones and joints

Parts of the digestive system

Your digestive system is like a long tube that is folded inside your body. When you swallow your food, it passes down the oesophagus (food pipe) into your stomach, where it is churned and mixed into a pulp. The stomach also secretes acids and other chemicals to dissolve your food. The soupy food then moves into your small and large intestine, where nutrients are passed into the bloodstream. Your liver, gall bladder and pancreas also supply chemicals that help in the digestive process.

Liver

Oesophagus (food pipe)

Stomach

Large intestine

Small intestine

Time chewing and swallowing

Time in stomach

Time in small intestine

Time in large intestine

Time to digest

Food takes up to 24 hours to pass through your digestive system. Although chewing and swallowing take a minute or so, your food will spend up to four hours in your stomach. Half-digested food then spends up to four hours in your small intestine, and up to 16 hours in the large intestine while all the nutrients are absorbed. The leftover waste is then expelled when you go to the toilet.

Why do we eat and drink?

Make a good start to the day by fueling your body! A varied breakfast provides the nourishment you need to get you on your way.

Your body needs food and fluids to grow and to maintain your body cells. But the food you eat has to be broken down into tiny pieces before your body can absorb the nutrients it contains. The digestive system works rather like a factory production line, with each part carrying out a step in the process. However, rather than assembling parts, the digestive system is a destruction line, which takes your food apart!

Goodness in food

Eating well is one of the most important things you can do to keep your body healthy. Nutrients are the useful parts of food. Your digestive system breaks down nutrients into pieces so small that they can pass through the lining of the digestive tube into your blood. They are then carried away to be used as fuel for energy, or to become part of you!

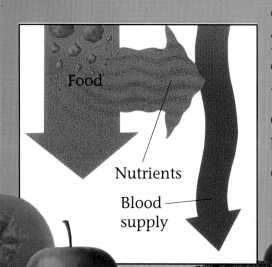

Food

Nutrients

Blood supply

Watery body

Believe it or not, your body is two-thirds water! This water level must be maintained if you are to stay in good health. Every day, your body loses about two litres of water as you sweat, breathe and go to the toilet. But you top up your water content by drinking liquids and eating food.

66.7 %

Eating a wide variety of different foods will keep your body in tiptop condition.

Regular meals

Your body needs regular nourishment throughout the day. It's better to eat moderate meals at regular intervals than to eat very little during the day and then have one big meal in the evening. If you give your body time to rest during and after your meals, your food will also be easier to digest.

Water world

Drinking water is the best way to give your body the water it needs. All your body cells are made up of water. Without it, your body cells become dehydrated and cannot work properly to keep your body healthy.

Feeling thirsty

Your body loses a lot of water when you sweat in hot weather and when you exercise. It's especially important to drink lots of water at these times. Feeling thirsty is your body's way of saying it needs more water!

7

Why do we get hungry?

Food is the fuel your body needs to keep going, just as a car needs petrol to zip along.

Food provides your body with the nutrients that it needs to power the hundreds of different chemical processes that go on in your body every minute of the day. When this fuel is running low, you will start to feel hungry. This is your body's way of telling you that you need more food.

Food for energy

Your body converts food into energy which it uses to keep active and healthy. The chart below shows the amount of energy each body part uses when you are resting. When you are active and moving about, the proportions change, because parts such as your muscles and heart use up more energy.

Your brain, liver and muscles are energy-hungry organs. They each use a fifth of the energy you need when resting. Your heart, kidneys, fat and other tissues use the remainder.

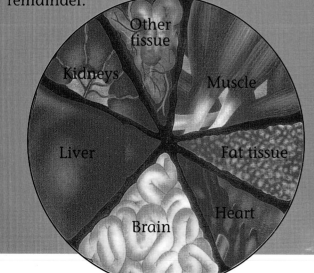

Other tissue

Kidneys

Muscle

Liver

Fat tissue

Brain

Heart

Body heat

Humans and other warm-blooded animals use a lot of energy to keep their bodies at a regular temperature, whatever the weather. Your body temperature remains constant at 37°C. If you are ill with a fever, your temperature will rise.

37°C

Food shortages

The human body needs nourishment to keep active and healthy. In poor parts of the world, many people are malnourished (underfed or poorly fed). If you are malnourished, your body is less able to fight infection. Every day about 830 million people are underfed. Meanwhile, obesity levels are rising in other parts of the world, where people are eating more than they need.

Food for growth

As you grow, your body uses nutrients and raw materials from your food to make new body tissues, including bones and muscles. Even when you are fully grown, your body still needs these raw materials to replace worn-out cells, and to repair injuries if you get hurt. However, if you eat more food than your body needs for energy and growth, your body will store the excess food as fat.

Calories

Energy in food is measured in units called calories. Your body uses different amounts of energy depending on whether you are active or at rest. When you are asleep, your body uses about one calorie a minute to keep your heart beating, your lungs working and your brain ticking over. Walking uses five calories per minute. You use 10 calories per minute when you go jogging and 20 calories per minute when you do more vigorous exercise.

Open wide

Chewing breaks down food for the next stage of the digestive process. A thorough chewing also gives you time to enjoy the taste of your food!

Your mouth is the starting point for your food's long journey through the digestive system. The mouth has a variety of specialised tools – including lips, teeth, tongue and saliva – that prepare your food for digestion. Together, these tools convert large, dry or crunchy food into small, soft, soggy lumps that can pass easily through your throat. Your tongue is also covered with taste buds that make your food enjoyable and can alert you if your food is bad.

Food processor

Each part of your mouth plays an important role in the early stages of the digestion process. Your lips open to take in food and then seal shut to prevent it from dribbling out. Your teeth bite off chunks of food and break them into smaller pieces.

Your tongue pushes food around to reach your teeth and is covered with sensitive taste buds to pick up salty, sweet, sour and bitter tastes.

Three pairs of glands produce saliva, a watery substance that moistens your food so you can swallow it. Saliva also contains amylase – a chemical that helps to break down food.

Salivary glands

Tongue

Teeth

Lips

Ready to eat

The smell or even just the thought of your favourite food can cause your salivary glands to produce saliva so that your mouth is ready to eat. Strangely enough, the smell of food you don't like doesn't produce the same effect!

Beware of germs

Hygiene (cleanliness) is very important around food because germs can make you ill if they enter your digestive system. Always wash your hands to get rid of germs before touching food. Insects like flies can carry germs, and there are also germs in the air. Food left outside the fridge or larder should be covered to keep germs out.

Food and health

Restaurants, cafés and other public food outlets have to take special care to maintain clean conditions. The government sets standards of hygiene and makes rules about food preparation. Health inspectors visit food outlets regularly to check that the standards are being met. They check the cleanliness of kitchen areas and the temperatures at which food is being stored and served (below).

Biting

The muscles connecting your jaws are some of the strongest muscles in your body. They allow you to bite on hard, crispy foods, such as apples. Your lower jaw is hinged to your skull so that you can open your mouth wide to take a big bite.

A bite to eat

You are the proud owner of two sets of teeth during your lifetime. Your first set of 20 baby (or milk) teeth is gradually replaced by a full set of 32 adult teeth.

Your teeth are the main tools you use to break down food in the first stage of the digestive process. You have different kinds of teeth to help you chop, slice, rip, tear, grind and crush the different types of food that you eat. Teeth are tough, bone-like structures. They are strong enough to crush even hard food, such as raw carrots.

Canine

Premolars

Molars

Incisor

Gums

Types of teeth

Your mouth holds four different sorts of teeth. The wide, chisel-shaped incisors at the front of your mouth are designed for chopping and slicing. Next to them, the sharp, pointed canines are used for ripping and tearing. The molars and premolars at the back are good for grinding and crushing food.

Baby teeth

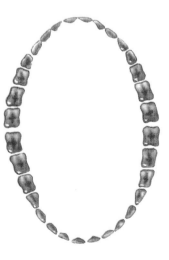

Adult teeth

Caring for your teeth

Your teeth will last a lifetime if you take good care of them. Brushing and flossing will remove leftover food and germs. Toothpastes containing fluoride help to strengthen your teeth and prevent tooth decay. Cutting down on sugary foods and drinks will also protect your teeth – sugars react with bacteria in your mouth to form an acid that causes tooth decay.

Teeth through life

Your first set of baby teeth began to form even before you were born. Between the age of six and twelve, these teeth fall out and are replaced by adult teeth. However, many adults don't have a full set of teeth because their rear molars, called 'wisdom teeth', never break through their gums.

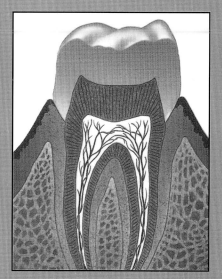

Strong roots

Your teeth are anchored in the jaw by strong roots and a bony glue called cement. Front teeth have just one root, but back teeth have two or even three.

Crown

The outer layer of a tooth, called the crown, is made of tough white enamel. This is the hardest material in your body – even harder than your bones.

Dentine

Below the crown is a bony layer of dentine. This softer layer is designed to absorb knocks and shocks.

Pulp cavity

Below the dentine, the soft pulp cavity inside the tooth contains blood vessels that provide nourishment. If the tooth becomes decayed, nerve endings in the pulp cavity can cause toothache.

Root

Down the hatch

When you have chewed your food thoroughly, it is ready to enter the next part of your digestive system. When you swallow, your food passes down the oesophagus (or food pipe) in your throat. The throat also contains the trachea (or windpipe), which takes the air that you breathe into your lungs. Luckily, your body has a built-in mechanism that makes sure that your food and air go down the right way!

Swallowing

The oesophagus is a stretchy tube about 25 cm long and 2.5 cm wide. When you are ready to swallow, your tongue presses food against the roof of your mouth to form a soft lump, and then nudges it into the upper throat. A flap called the epiglottis drops down over the trachea at this moment to prevent food going down the wrong pipe.

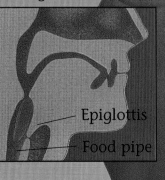

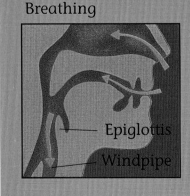

Breathing

Eating

Epiglottis

Windpipe

Epiglottis

Food pipe

14

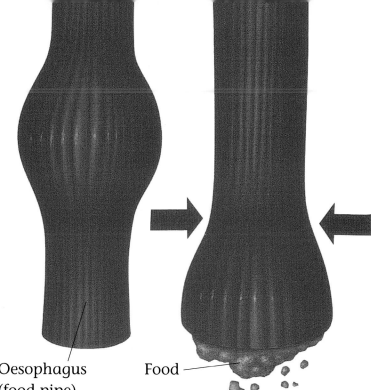

Oesophagus
(food pipe)   Food

Peristalsis

When you eat, the muscular walls of your oesophagus relax in front of your food, creating a wide opening, and squeeze together behind it. This process (called peristalsis) has the effect of nudging your food along. Peristalsis happens not just in your oesophagus, but in many other parts of the body. For example, food is pushed right through the digestive tract by muscular walls contracting in the same way.

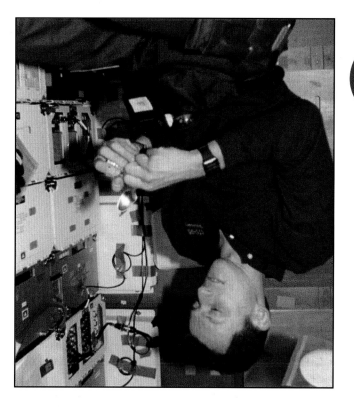

Any way up

Food is pushed along your oesophagus by muscular activity, not gravity. This means that it is possible to eat or even drink while standing on your head, although you are quite likely to choke if you try! The process of peristalsis enables astronauts, who are floating about in spacecraft beyond the pull of gravity, to eat their food.

Choking

Chewing your food thoroughly will enable you to swallow your food comfortably. Chewed food also has a greater surface area, so your digestive system can work more effectively at breaking your food down. If your food goes down your windpipe and you start to choke, you will usually be able to dislodge the obstruction by coughing. Very rarely, a piece of food can completely block the windpipe. If this happens, an adult can help you to breathe by performing the Heimlich manoeuvre – clasping you under your diaphragm and squeezing suddenly. This forces out a blast of air to free the obstruction.

15

In your stomach

When you are hungry, your stomach may rumble as it churns gas and digestive juices, ready to tackle your next meal.

Your stomach is your food's first major stop on its journey. Shaped like a boxing glove, the stretchy bag of your stomach expands to hold the food and drink you have consumed, while its muscular walls squeeze and churn your food into a soupy mush. Meanwhile, the lining of the stomach releases acid and other digestive juices that kill germs and help to dissolve your food.

Food allergies

An allergy occurs when your body reacts abnormally to otherwise harmless substances. An allergic reaction to food may cause stomach pains or skin rashes. Many different types of food can cause allergies; nuts, dairy products, and wheat are common troublemakers. Some people are allergic to chemicals called additives, which are put into processed foods to preserve them – making them look and taste good.

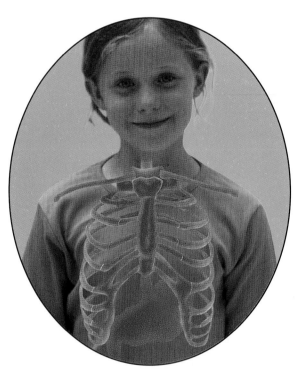

Where is your stomach?
Your stomach lies just below your rib cage. It is the widest part of your digestive system and can hold about 1.5 litres (3 pints). Although your stomach contains strong acids, it doesn't dissolve itself. This is because it has a strong protective lining of cells that renew themselves every few days.

Step by step

The stomach acts as a food mixer and blender. Food entering the stomach is squeezed to a pulp by the muscular walls. Some simple sugars are absorbed into your bloodstream directly through the stomach wall, while powerful chemicals, called enzymes, help to dissolve the rest of your food. After about an hour, the pulp has dissolved into a creamy soup called chyme (1). Up to four hours later, the half-digested food is ready to pass to your small intestine (2). A ring of muscle (pyloric muscle) that bars the stomach's exit now relaxes and opens at regular intervals, allowing half-digested food to pass through to the small intestine (3).

Pyloric muscle

❶

❷

❸

Your small intestine

Runny, half-digested food leaves your stomach by passing into the small intestine – a very long, thin tube coiled inside your abdomen. Your food spends up to four hours in your small intestine. Nutrients from your food pass through the lining of the intestinal tube to be processed by the liver. These nutrients then travel through the bloodstream to help maintain body cells, or to be converted into energy.

The 'small' intestine is only a few centimetres wide, but is about 6 metres long – more than half the length of the whole digestive tract.

Small intestine

Parts of the small intestine

The long, thin small intestine can be divided into three sections. The first section, the duodenum, measures about 25 cm. Here, more digestive chemicals are added to food. The middle part, the jejunum, is 2.5 m long. The final section, the ileum, measures 3 m. In these last two sections, many nutrients from your food are absorbed into the body.

Fibre
Fibre is the indigestible part of food that gives it bulk. Fibre helps the digestive passages to grip food as it passes through the system and also softens the faeces. You can keep your digestive system healthy by eating food with plenty of fibre, such as leafy vegetables, fruit and wholemeal bread.

Energy source

The food that you eat helps your body to grow and maintain a number of vital body processes. Simple sugars in your food, like glucose, combine with oxygen in your body cells to create energy. This is the energy that helps your body to circulate your blood, activate your brain, maintain your body temperature and move your muscles when you play sport.

Absorbing nourishment

The small intestine is lined with thousands of tiny, finger-shaped projections called villi. These villi contain a network of blood vessels that absorb nutrients from your food. The tiny folds of villi increase the surface area of your intestine hundreds of times, to extract as many nutrients as possible. The nutrients are then carried away to be processed by the liver. Some are used as building blocks to grow and repair your cells; others are converted to energy so that your body can move and maintain a healthy temperature.

Muscly tube
Your small intestine includes two layers of muscle (right). This long, thin tube is folded many times (above), so that it will fit inside your abdomen.

Villi

Muscle layers

Villi

Blood vessels

Liver, pancreas and gall bladder

The liver stores nutrients, including sugar. This sugar can be saved until your body needs it, such as when you run a race.

The liver, pancreas and gall bladder are not part of the digestive passage, but they are important because they help to filter, store and prepare the nutrients that have passed through the small intestine. The liver and pancreas also do other important jobs in the body – the liver filters your blood to remove waste and the pancreas controls your blood sugar levels.

Location of the liver, pancreas and gall bladder

Your liver lies on the right side of your upper abdomen, partly in front of your stomach. It is tucked inside the bottom ribs, which protect it from injury, and has two parts called lobes. The gall bladder is tucked under the liver, and the long, slender pancreas lies just behind it. Tubes called ducts carry the digestive juices produced by these organs into the small intestine.

◎ Dangers of alcohol

One of the liver's jobs is to break down harmful substances in the body, such as alcohol. Drinking too much alcohol can damage your liver so that it can't break down wastes properly. If this happens, poisons build up in your body. Alcohol can also damage other parts of your body, including the heart and brain.

Liver

Pancreas

Gall Bladder

Liver and gall bladder

Your liver does many vital jobs for your body. It receives nutrient-rich blood from the small intestine and filters it to remove waste. It also stores excess glucose (sugar) and starch, for when your body needs them, such as when you play energetic games. The liver also stores other nutrients, such as iron, that your body needs, and breaks down old blood cells to recycle the useful parts they contain. One chemical that is broken down from your blood is bilirubin. This forms a yellowish liquid, called bile, which is then stored in your gall bladder. When you digest more food, this bile is released into the small intestine, where it helps to digest fatty foods.

Right liver lobe

Blood vessels

Left liver lobe

Pancreatic ducts

Gall bladder   Bile duct

Diabetes

Diabetes is a condition that occurs when the pancreas doesn't make enough insulin or when the body doesn't use insulin effectively. People with diabetes have to monitor how much sugar they eat. Some can be treated with medications that help the body to use insulin more effectively. Others need daily injections of insulin.

The pancreas

The pancreas makes digestive juices that help to break down proteins in your food. The pancreas also makes insulin, the hormone that enables your body cells to use and store the glucose (sugar) you have eaten in your food, to give you energy.

Your large intestine

Your large intestine is a muscular tube that receives digested food from your small intestine. It continues the digestive process by absorbing remaining nutrients and water from your food. During this process your undigested food becomes more solid. The solid waste, called faeces, is stored in your large intestine and passes out of your body when you go to the toilet.

Minerals, like iron and calcium, are absorbed in the large intestine to keep your body healthy. Drinking milk and eating a varied diet should supply you with all the minerals you need.

End of the line

Undigested waste passes along your large intestine as the muscle walls contract regularly. The tube lining produces slippery mucus that eases the waste along. Faeces are stored in the rectum until you go to the toilet. They then pass out of the body through the muscular ring of the anus.

Three parts

Your large intestine is made up of three main sections: the caecum, colon and rectum. The caecum is a pouch where the end of the lower small intestine meets the large intestine. A finger-like organ called the appendix leads from it. The colon forms the main length of the large intestine. It ends in another pouch, the rectum, where waste is stored.

Large intestine

Rectum

Digestive illnesses

Many kinds of bacteria live in your digestive system to help process your food. Digestive illnesses are causd by viral infections or by 'bad' bacteria that grow in spoiled food. Occasionally, parasites, like threadworms or tapeworms, can enter the digestive system. Tapeworms (right) are more common in tropical regions. These parasites grow in the large intestine and use nutrients that are needed by your body. Washing your hands after going to the toilet and before preparing food will help prevent infections of this kind.

Water and minerals

Colon

Caecum

Appendix

The large intestine

The large intestine encloses the small intestine like a frame around a picture. It is wider than the small intestine, about 5 cm wide, but much shorter, only about 1.5 m.

Rectum

Anus

Dead end
The appendix is a tiny, closed tube coming from the caecum. It seems to have no part in the digestive process but if it gets blocked by waste, it may become inflamed and infected. This condition is called appendicitis. In many cases the appendix may have to be removed in a surgical operation.

Antibiotics
Antibiotics are medicines that treat infections caused by 'bad' bacteria. However, antibiotics also kill the 'good' bacteria in your body and may cause digestive upsets like stomach pains or diarrhoea. Eating foods that are rich in 'good' bacteria, such as yoghurt and cottage cheese, can counteract the problem.

Body wastes

Just as a wood fire sends some materials into the air as smoke and gases, leaving a residue of ash, your body's digestive system leaves waste behind once it has extracted the goodness it needs. Solid wastes from the digestive system are passed from the body as faeces. The kidneys also work to filter your blood, taking out extra water and impurities. You pass this waste from your body as urine.

Vomiting is a way your body can get rid of spoiled food and bad bacteria. It may not be pleasant, but it's better out than in!

Faeces

Brownish faeces are the leftovers of the digestive process. They are mainly indigestible food remains, or roughage, and a little water. Faeces also contain tiny bits of intestine lining and dead bacteria. After going to the toilet, always wash your hands carefully with soap and water, to get rid of harmful germs.

Kidneys

Bladder

Urine

Your kidneys lie just behind your stomach and liver. They filter your blood to clean it. The waste product of this process, urine, trickles down to collect in your bladder and leaves your body via a tube called the urethra.

Open sewers

Rich countries of the world have well-developed sewage systems that carry away and process human waste to prevent disease from spreading. In poor countries, open sewers can spread diseases such as cholera and dysentery – these infections of the digestive system may be spread in dirty drinking water.

The runs
Diarrhoea, sometimes called 'the runs', is passing semi-liquid faeces. It may be caused by an infection, eating contaminated food, or just anxiety or excitement. Luckily, you rarely eat food that is contaminated because your body has inbuilt defence mechanisms of smell and taste, to warn you if your food has gone off. At the opposite end of the scale, constipation occurs when your faeces become so hard that they are painful to pass. Some people empty their bowels two or three times a day, others only every other day or so.

Natural remedies

Many people believe that eating certain foods can clear up or prevent digestive problems. Bananas are thought to help cure diarrhoea. Food that contains lots of fibre, such as breakfast cereals containing bran (below), can soften the faeces and ease constipation.

Sensible eating

Eat five helpings of fruits and vegetables every day to keep your body in top shape.

A healthy diet contains three main kinds of nourishment: carbohydrates, proteins and fats. These foods give your body energy and help your body to grow and repair cells and tissues.

Your body also needs small amounts of natural substances, called minerals and vitamins.

A balanced diet should provide your body with all the nutrients that it needs.

Carbohydrates

Starchy or sugary foods, like rice, pasta, bread, potatoes, cereals and fruit, are rich in carbohydrates. Your body breaks these down to sugar, which gives you energy.

Fats and oils

Fats and oils provide your body with energy and help it grow and maintain itself. Dairy produce, nuts, plant oils, meat and fish are fatty or oily foods.

Proteins

Proteins are used to make the basic framework of your body, including bones and muscles. Meat, fish, eggs, dairy products, beans and nuts are protein-rich foods.

Fruit for life

Fruit is one of the healthiest foods to eat. Fruit contains sugar, minerals and water – many of the vital nutrients that your body needs to stay healthy.

Food pyramid

Your body needs different amounts of nutrients to stay healthy. The correct proportions form a pyramid shape, shown opposite. At the base, the main ingredients of a balanced diet are carbohydrates, fruit and vegetables. Your body needs a smaller amount of animal protein, and at the top of the pyramid, only a small quantity of fats and oils.

Healthy balance

Eating too much of the same foods, particularly sweet things, can make you feel sick. Even healthy foods, like fruit and vegetables, should be varied so that you get all the vitamins and minerals you need.

Junk food

Eating a few 'junk foods', such as burgers and chips, probably won't harm you. But these high-fat foods are unhealthy if they are eaten regularly in large amounts. A high-fat diet can increase your blood pressure, make you put on weight, and cause heart disease and other serious illnesses.

Fibre

Fruit, vegetables, wholemeal bread, cereals, beans and lentils all contain fibre. You need to eat plenty of fibre to keep your digestive system working well.

Vitamins

Your body needs small amounts of vitamins – natural substances that help to keep the body healthy – such as vitamin C, which is found in citrus fruits, tomatoes and even potatoes! A balanced diet will supply most people with all the vitamins they need.

Fats and oils

Animal proteins

Carbohydrates

Fruit and vegetables

Take time to eat

Help your digestive system to tackle your food by sitting down to eat and resting for a while after a big meal. Eating 'on the go', or being active too soon after a meal, may give you cramp or indigestion. So take it easy – give your body time to digest!

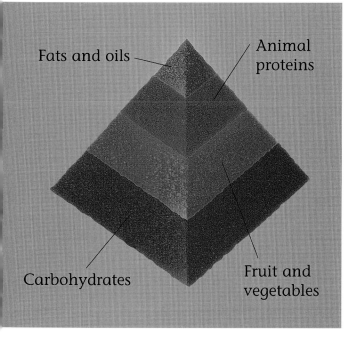

Staying healthy

Your digestive system is a very clever design of different body processes, but you can do many things yourself to keep this system working effectively. By taking care with the food that you eat and keeping yourself in good general health, you can ensure that you get the best from your digestive system and lead a full and active life.

Get active

Regular exercise uses food to make energy that would otherwise be stored as fat. Any kind of exercise that gets your heart beating faster and your lungs working burns energy. This helps keep your body in good shape.

Eat for life

Eating a wide variety of foods and drinking plenty of water will help keep your digestive system and your whole body in top condition. Fibre-rich fruit and vegetables are particularly good for digestion. If you feel hungry between meals, try a fruit or a cereal bar snack instead of crisps and sweets.

Tooth check
Tooth decay and gum disease are among the world's most common health problems! Regular trips to the dentist can prevent these problems from developing or quickly repair them.

Thirst quencher

It's important to constantly add fresh water to your body. Water is required by every cell in your body and helps many body systems work efficiently.

In the mood

Eating a balanced diet will help you feel your best! Researchers have found that some of the nutrients in the food that you eat can affect your brain. Proteins, like meat, are thought to make you more alert, while carbohydrates, like pasta, are thought to be good for relaxation.

Weight

Maintaining a healthy body weight is important if you want to keep fit and healthy. If you are too thin, your immune system will become weak and you will be less able to fight infections. Eating too little will also leave you with little energy and may mean that your body is unable to carry out vital body processes. Overeating, on the other hand, increases the amount of fat in your body, putting a strain on your heart and increasing your blood pressure. Try to eat a sensible, balanced diet.

One of a kind

The human body comes in many different shapes and sizes – it's natural. Some people need to eat more than others to maintain their body weight and keep themselves healthy. Don't worry if you are taller, shorter, bigger or smaller than some of your friends. The chances are, your body shape is right for you.

Amazing facts

Your body needs from 15 to 20 different vitamins to stay healthy and fight off diseases. For example, a disease called scurvy is caused by a lack of vitamin C. It was common among old-time sailors who lived for months at sea, without fresh fruits or vegetables.

Your food travels 25 cm down your oesophagus, before it reaches your stomach – the first major stop in the digestive system. After this your food still has another 7.5 metres to travel.

You need to take in over two litres of water each day to maintain your body's water level. Two-thirds of this total comes from the liquids you drink. Most of the rest comes from your food.

Although your whole body is made of two-thirds water, your blood is made of eight-tenths water and your brain is made of seven-tenths water.

The finger-like villi in your small intestine are only 1 mm long, but together they form a nourishment-absorbing surface that is 20 times the size of your skin!

Glossary

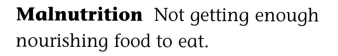

Bile A yellowish liquid produced by the liver, which helps your digestive system break down fats.

Calorie A unit for measuring the amount of energy in food.

Diabetes An illness in which the level of glucose (sugar) in the blood is not properly controlled by the body. Many diabetics do not have enough insulin, a hormone made by the pancreas.

Digestion The process in which food is broken down and the nourishment it contains is absorbed to become part of the body.

Energy The invisible force that makes things work. Machines get energy from fuel; humans and other animals get energy from their food.

Enzyme A substance that is needed for a chemical reaction to take place in the body. Digestive enzymes help the digestive process by breaking down particles of food.

Hormone A body substance that acts as a chemical messenger, instructing cells or organs to work in a particular way.

Malnutrition Not getting enough nourishing food to eat.

Nutrients The nourishment or useful parts in food.

Oesophagus The food pipe that carries food and liquid to the stomach.

Organ A body part with a distinct function, such as the heart or brain.

Peristalsis The wave-like movement made by the muscular walls of the digestive passage, which pushes food along.

Trachea [windpipe] The pipe that carries air to the lungs.

Villi [sing. villus] The tiny finger-like projections that form a frilly lining to the small intestine and absorb the nutrients from food.

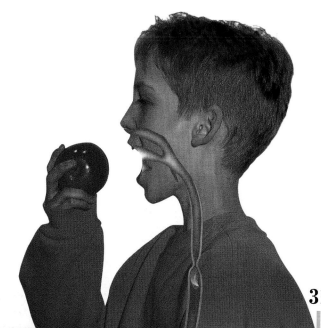

Index

Photo credits

Abbreviations: l-left, r-right, b-bottom, t-top, c-centre, m-middle

All photos supplied by Select Pictures except for: 4mr, 6b all, 7ml, 16ml, 16bl both, 30tl – Stockbyte. 7bl – Corel. 9tr – Peter Turnley/CORBIS. 11mr – Antonia Reeve/Science Photo Library. 15ml – NASA. 19tr – Paul A. Souders/CORBIS. 25tr – David Nunuk/Science Photo Library. 27tr – USDA. 28c, 29l – Digital Stock.